MA+H
EVERYWHERE

1493

D0862295

FRACTION FRENZY

Fractions and Decimals

Rob Colson

Children's Press®
An Imprint of Scholastic Inc.

1/19

Acknowledgments and Photo Credits

Library of Congress Cataloging-in-Publication Data
A CIP catalog record for this book is available from the Library of Congress.

No part of this publication may be reproduced in whole or in part, or stored in a
retrieval system, or transmitted in any form or by any means, electronic, mechanical,
photocopying, recording, or otherwise, without written permission of the publisher.
For information regarding permission, write to Scholastic Inc., Attention: Permissions
Department, 557 Broadway, New York, NY 10012.

Copyright © The Watts Publishing Group, 2016
First published by Franklin Watts 2016
Published in the United States by Scholastic Inc. 2018

All rights reserved.

Printed in Shenzhen, China

SCHOLASTIC, CHILDREN'S PRESS, and associated logos are trademarks and/or
registered trademarks of Scholastic Inc.

2 3 4 5 6 7 8 9 10 R 27 26 25 24 23 22 21 20 19 18

Photo credits:
t-top, b-bottom, l-left, r-right, c-center, front cover-fc, back cover-bc
All images courtesy of Dreamstime.com, unless indicated:
Inside front Jefunne; fc, bc Pablo631; fctr Mycoolsites; fcc Artigiano; fcbl Kakigori;
1c, 22b Peter Bertok; 4, 28b Burlesck; 5b Skripko Ievgen; 5b Ahmet Ihsan Ariturk;
6, 22tl Photka; 7br Maxim Popov; 8t Mirko Milutinovic; 8br, 31tr Cjansuebsri; 9c
Aremac; 9cr Wuka; 9bl Stefanschurr226; 9br Franz Pfluegl; 10l Kmiragaya; 11tr
Nakedcm; 11c, 29tr Macrolink; 11b, 23b Mexrix; 11br Hvat10; 12b Chaoss; 13c
Winnond; 13bl Jordygraph; bctr, 14br Ronstik; 15t Vectorverde; 15bl Szefei; fccl, 16b
Liligraphie; bccr, 17tr Matriyoshka; 19b Luislouro; fcbr, 20l Mikkel Strøbech; fccr,
20tl Martin Malchev; fcc, 20tc Shaeree Mukherjee; 23b Stoupa; 23br NASA; bctl,
24-25t Katrina Brown; bctl, 24-25t Wolfgangbeyer; 25br Oleksandr Solonenko; 27
Andreadonetti; 29b Luanateutzi; fctc, 30t Fotosv; 30b Alexmoe; 32t Stylephotographs

Teaching Guide

Visit this Scholastic Web site to download the
Teaching Guide for this series:
www.factsfornow.scholastic.com
Enter the keywords **Fraction Frenzy**

MIX
Paper from
responsible sources
FSC
www.fsc.org
FSC® C104740

Scholastic Inc., 557 Broadway, New York, NY 10012.

Contents

What Is a Fraction?

A fraction is part of a whole. The word *fraction* comes from the Latin word *frangere*, meaning "to break." A fraction is one number that has been broken up by another.

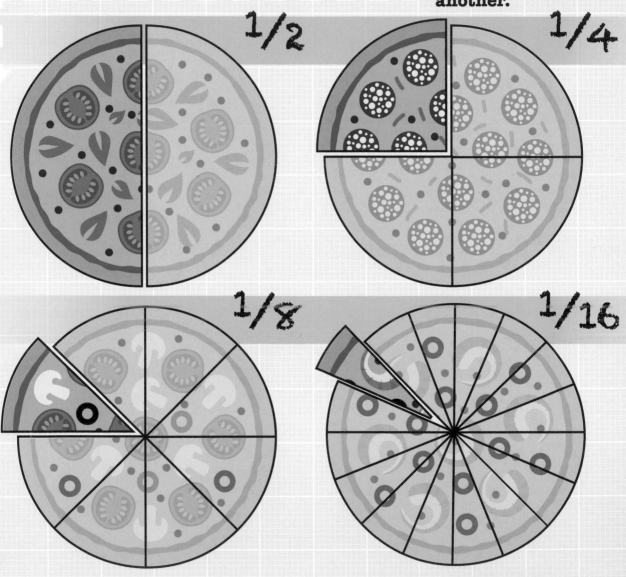

1/2

1/4

1/8

1/16

A fraction is written using two numbers. The top number, called the numerator, is the number of pieces we have. The bottom number, called the denominator, is the number of pieces in the whole.

numerator

3/8

denominator

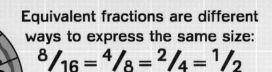

Equivalent fractions are different ways to express the same size:

$$^8/_{16} = \, ^4/_8 = \, ^2/_4 = \, ^1/_2$$

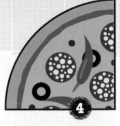

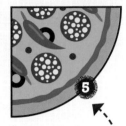

8/16

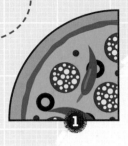

4/8

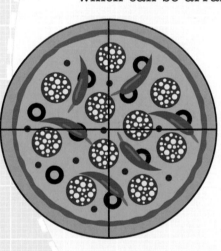

2/4

Improper Fractions

Improper fractions represent more than a whole. For example, $^5/_4$ is **five-quarters**, which can be arranged to make **1** and $^1/_4$.

1/2

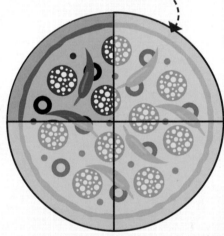

Ancient Fractions

The ancient Romans wrote fractions using multiples of twelfths, such as $^1/_{12}$, $^1/_{24}$, or $^1/_{144}$. They would think of $^1/_2$ as **six-twelfths**, and it was called a **semi**. The ancient Babylonians wrote fractions as the number of sixtieths, so $^1/_2$ would be **30-sixtieths**.

Back around AD 500, people in India became the first to write out fractions using a numerator and a denominator. Later, Arab scholars added a line between the two. This system was flexible because you could use any number as the denominator.

Sums with Fractions

Adding fractions

Adding fractions with the same denominator is easy.

$$\frac{1}{6} + \frac{3}{6} = \frac{4}{6}$$

Where the denominators are different, you first need to find a common denominator. The simplest way to do this is to multiply the denominators together.

(Numerator A) x (Denominator B)
1 x 6

(Numerator B) x (Denominator A)
1 x 5

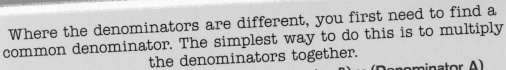

$$\underset{A}{\frac{1}{5}} + \underset{B}{\frac{1}{6}} = \frac{6}{30} + \frac{5}{30} = \frac{11}{30}$$

5 x 6
(Denominator A) x (Denominator B)

Often the answer can be simplified. Here is an example:

$$\frac{3}{8} + \frac{1}{6} = \frac{18}{48} + \frac{8}{48} = \frac{26}{48}$$

Dividing both numerator and denominator by **2** gives $\frac{13}{24}$ so **24** is the **lowest common denominator**.

Subtraction

Subtracting fractions is very similar to addition. Find a common denominator and subtract one numerator from the other:

(2 x 4)   (1 x 5)

$$\frac{2}{5} - \frac{1}{4} = \frac{8 - 5}{20}$$

$$= \frac{3}{20}$$

(5 x 4)

Multiplying

Multiplying fractions can be summed up as:

$$\frac{\text{Top times top}}{\text{Bottom times bottom}}$$

For example: $3/5 \times 7/9 = (3 \times 7)/(5 \times 9) = 21/45$

You may need to simplify to find the **lowest denominator**. In this instance, you can divide both numerator and denominator by **3**:

$$21/45 = 7/15$$

Division

Division is almost as easy as multiplication. Turn the second fraction upside down and multiply:

$$2/5 \div 3/4 = 2/5 \times 4/3 = (2 \times 4)/(5 \times 3) = 8/15$$

4/3 is called the **reciprocal** of $3/4$: $3/4 \times 4/3 = 12/12 = 1$
Any number **multiplied** by its reciprocal **equals 1**.

"Line up, everything is $1/2$ price!"

Pete is looking to set up a market stand to sell fruits and vegetables, but he's not sure whether it is worth it.

He must give $1/3$ of his earnings to the supplier and then a further $1/4$ to pay rent for the market stand.

After paying his expenses, what fraction of his earnings is left as profit?

To work out how much of his earnings Pete will have in profit, subtract his expenses from 1:
$$1 - 1/3 - 1/4$$

Find a common denominator by multiplying $3 \times 4 = 12$. That makes:
$$12/12 - 4/12 - 3/12 = 5/12$$
So Pete will keep $5/12$ of his earnings as profit.

Fractions to Decimals

A decimal is a way of writing a number in base 10. Each digit in a decimal number represents a multiple or fraction of ten.

Decimal point

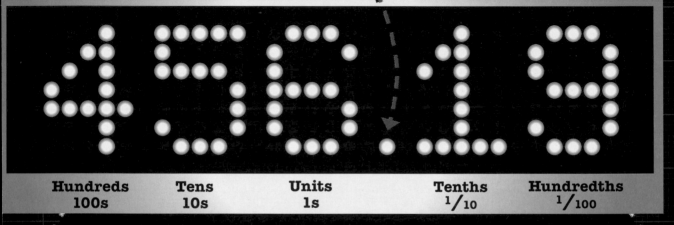

Hundreds 100s	Tens 10s	Units 1s	Tenths $1/10$	Hundredths $1/100$

The **decimal point** shows the space between the whole units and the tenths. A decimal fraction is a fraction with a denominator that is a **multiple of ten**:
$$6/10 = 0.6, \quad 43/100 = 0.43, \quad 125/1000 = 0.125$$

To convert a fraction to a decimal, you first need to find an equivalent fraction with a denominator that is a multiple of 10. For example:
$$1/5 = 2/10 = 0.2, \quad 1/4 = 25/100 = 0.25$$
Sometimes, you cannot make an exact decimal from a fraction. For example, converting $1/3$ to a decimal produces 0.333..., where **...** means "**recurring.**" This means the **threes go on forever**.
Other recurring decimals include:
$$1/9 = 0.111... \text{ (1 repeating)}$$
$$1/11 = 0.090909... \text{ (09 repeating)}$$

Calculators use decimal fractions. At some point, the calculator needs to **round** a recurring decimal to the nearest decimal place. This means that you round the last digit **down** if the next digit is **under 5**, and **up** if the next digit is **5 or more**. For example, to five decimal places, $1/3 = 0.33333$ and $1/11 = 0.09091$.

0.3333333

Stop the Clock!

Sprint races, like the 100m, are timed to the nearest

1/100

(0.01) of a second. The starter fires a gun to start the race. This sends an electric signal to start the timer. At the finish line, a high-speed camera pointing straight across the line captures the moment when the athletes cross it. Some part of the torso must cross the line to count as having finished, stopping the clock.

A composite photo shows all the finishers in a 100-meter race. The lines show the moment they stopped the clock.

9.96 seconds

10.23 seconds

9.85 seconds

10.29 seconds

10.08 seconds

10.13 seconds

9.91 seconds

10.06 seconds

10.4 10.3 10.2 10.1 10.0 9.9 9.8

False Start

Pressure-sensitive starting blocks sense when the athletes start to move. A false start is recorded if any athlete moves before the gun or up to 0.1 ($1/10$) of a second after the gun.

Starting block

Firing of gun

Signal from brain to legs

Sound to ear
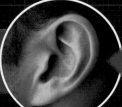

Scientists have calculated that it is impossible for the ear to hear a sound and the brain to send a signal to the muscles in less than this time. So if an athlete moves, say, 0.05 ($5/100$) of a second after the gun, he or she must have anticipated the start before the gun sounded.

Egyptian Fractions

The ancient Egyptians wrote every fraction as the sum of a series of fractions with the numerator 1. These are called reciprocals, or unit fractions, and the Egyptians wrote them like this.

$2 = 1/2$

$3 = 1/3$

$5 = 1/5$

Each fraction in the series to be added had to be different. So, for example:

$2/3$ could not be $1/3 + 1/3$

Instead it was:

$$2/3 = 1/2 + 1/6 \text{ or}$$
$$2/3 = 1/3 + 1/4 + 1/12$$

Or you could make a really long series like this:

$$2/3 = 1/4 + 1/7 + 1/12 +$$
$$1/13 + 1/21 + 1/31 + 1/42$$
$$+ 1/156 + 1/420 + 1/930$$

In fact, for every fraction, there is an infinite number of different Egyptian fraction series!

Egyptian fractions are very useful when working out equal portions. The Egyptians used them to divide their bread rations.

"Hey, hands off."

For example, if you have eight workers but just five loaves, **how do you divide the bread equally** among your workers? You could slice each of the five loaves into eight pieces. The workers would get five slices each. However, using Egyptian fractions can give you a better solution:

$$5/8 = 1/2 + 1/8$$

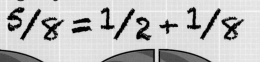

So you slice one loaf into eight and the other four into half. Each worker gets two pieces— $1/2$ and $1/8$. That's less slicing and fewer crumbs than five $1/8$s!

Smart Thinking

Old Josiah has three children, Agnes, Jake, and Patrick. He also has 12 prize horses. In his will he leaves $1/2$ of his horses to Agnes, $1/3$ to Jake, and $1/12$ to Patrick. However, Old Josiah dies in a riding accident that also kills one of his horses, leaving just 11 to be inherited. Patrick is to be left $1/12$ of the horses, which is just $11/12$ of a horse!

How could they solve their problem?

Old Josiah's lawyer, Frances, comes up with the solution. She adds her own horse to the prize horses to bring the number back up to 12. Now the inheritance can be decided exactly:

Agnes gets $1/2 \times 12$ = 6 horses
Jake gets $1/3 \times 12$ = 4 horses
Patrick gets $1/12 \times 12$ = 1 horse

That's a total of 11 horses, so Frances takes her horse back home with her and everyone is happy. It turns out that when he was writing his will, Old Josiah added slightly wrong:

$$1/2 + 1/3 + 1/12 = 11/12, \text{ not } 12/12$$

Irrational Numbers

What is the square root of 2?

In the sixth century BC, a group of Greek mathematicians thought they had discovered a beautiful idea. Everything in the universe, they believed, could be described by whole numbers, either on their own or combined to make fractions. Their motto was:

"All is number."

One of the most famous proofs in math is named after the group's leader, Pythagoras. The Pythagorean theorem states: In a **right triangle**, the square of the hypotenuse **equals the sum** of **the squares** of the other two sides.

c^2

a^2 a c
b

b^2

$$a^2 + b^2 = c^2$$

? 1

1

One of Pythagoras's followers, Hippasus, asked the question: **What about a square with sides 1 unit long? What is the length of its diagonal?**

"Think of a number."

According to Pythagoras's theorem, the **length of the diagonal** equals $\sqrt{2}$—that's a number that, **multiplied by itself**, equals 2. It's a number between 1 and 2, but this was no problem for the Pythagoreans as long as they could write the **improper fraction** in the form a/b, **where *a* and *b* are whole numbers**. The problem was that Hippasus proved that you cannot do that. There are no values of a and b for which $a/b \times a/b = 2$.

Legend has it that the unfortunate Hippasus was drowned at sea because of his disturbing discovery. But he had made a huge contribution to mathematics—he had discovered irrational numbers, which are all the numbers that we cannot write as a/b.

"Uh, okay, irrational, whole, or incorrect?"

Irrationally Useful

It turns out that many of the most important numbers in math are irrational.

Pi (π) is the **ratio** of a circle's **circumference** to its **diameter**.
pi = 3.14159...

diameter

circumference

The number **e** is used in many branches of math. Known as the **exponential number**, it describes a phenomenon called *exponential growth*, in which the rate of growth increases as size increases.
e = 2.71828...

The Golden Ratio, **phi (φ)**, describes a **rectangle** in which the ratio between both of its sides added together and its longer side is **equal** to the ratio between the longer side and the shorter side.
phi = 1.61803...

1

1.61803...

Cracking
Combinations

While fractions break wholes into pieces, combinations put pieces together. The branch of math that deals with combinations is called *combinatorics*. We use this math to keep our secrets safe.

How secure is your lock?

On a combination lock using numbers, working out how many different combinations there are is reasonably easy. With four numbers, each from **0 to 9**, you have **10 different numbers** for each position, so there are

10 x 10 x 10 x 10 combinations, from

0000 to 9999. That's

10,000 combinations.

Each extra digit added to the lock multiplies the number of combinations by 10, so adding one digit makes the lock **10 times harder to crack**.

PASSWORD

When choosing a password for an Internet site, there is a choice between letters, digits, or symbols for each character. There are **26 letters** that can be upper- or lowercase, **10 digits**, and around **33 other symbols**. That makes

$$26 + 26 + 10 + 33 = 95$$

That means that for an eight-character password, there are

$$95 \times 95 \times 95 \times 95 \times 95 \times 95 \times 95 \times 95 = 95^8 =$$

6.6 quadrillion possibilities

(1 quadrillion = 1,000 trillion)

To make a secure password, you should choose a mix of characters at random. However, most of us choose passwords that we find memorable. The most popular eight-character password on the Internet is "**password**." The second most popular is "**12345678**." Other popular passwords include "**baseball**," "**football**," and pet names. Hackers make lists of popular combinations and try them out using computer programs. So to be safe, you will need to come up with something much more random.

For instance, the password below may be hard to remember, but it would also be impossible to guess:

4H_@jr8Q

A password of Fudge2009 might be cracked by a hacker if your dog is named Fudge, her birth year is 2009, and you posted pictures of her as a puppy on your social media page.

Secret Codes

Sending secret messages is called *cryptography*. A code is used to substitute one letter for another, and you make sense of the message by applying the code in reverse. For example, what might the code below mean?

OJKNZXMZO

Here, the code is a simple one: arrange all the letters in a line and move back five letters for each letter. When you reach A, go back to Z. Reversing the process to undo the code, you need to add five letters:

TOPSECRET

This is a type of *substitution cipher*, in which one letter is substituted for another according to a mathematical rule. In ancient Rome, Julius Caesar used this "shift" cipher to keep his messages secret.

You can make your own codes using whatever rules you like. As long as both you and the recipient of the message know the cipher, you both will be able to read it.

Factorization

Banks employ a far more secure form of encryption to protect their customers' money, using prime *factorization*. Prime factorization is the breaking down of a number into its prime factors. These are numbers that can only be divided by 1 and themselves. Factorizing small numbers is easy. For example:

$$15 = 3 \times 5$$
$$26 = 2 \times 13$$
$$84 = 2 \times 2 \times 3 \times 7$$
$$105 = 3 \times 5 \times 7$$

It is easy to make a large number out of its prime factors. For example:

$$2 \times 2 \times 3 \times 5 \times 11 \times 13 \times 17 \times 31 \times 79 \times 97$$
$$= 34{,}649{,}480{,}580$$

However, there is no easy way to work backward. Without knowing the answer, it takes a lot of computer power to factorize **34,649,480,580**. It is easy to make a number by multiplying primes that are 30 digits long, but it would take a computer billions of years of calculating to factorize it. Codes built by making large numbers out of prime factors are effectively unbreakable.

"You've got no chance, dude."

An Enigma machine

Cracking the Enigma Code

During World War II (1939–1945), the German army used a device called the Enigma machine to send secret radio messages. It used a combination of electrical wires and rotors to encode messages with 158,962,555,217,826,360,000 (nearly 159 quintillion) possible combinations.

British code breakers found repeated patterns in the Enigma messages that reduced the possible combinations down to a more manageable 100,000. They constructed a huge calculating machine, called the Bombe, which could work through combinations mechanically. Teams of workers put radio messages through the Bombe, and eventually they broke the code. The code breakers worked at Bletchley Park, an estate in England. They were led by the brilliant mathematician Alan Turing. Their role in helping to end the war remained a secret for many decades.

Numbers Going Bang!

To work out combinations of objects when we can only use each object once, we need an operation called a factorial.

In a classroom with **6 desks** and **6 pupils**, how many different ways can the pupils arrange themselves? Looking at each desk in turn, there are **6 choices** for the first desk. Once the first desk is taken, there are then **5 pupils** and **5 desks** left, so for each of the 6 choices for the first desk, there are 5 choices for the **second desk**. With the second desk filled, there are **4 choices** for the **third desk**, and so on all the way down to the last desk. The number of possible combinations is:

$$6 \times 5 \times 4 \times 3 \times 2 \times 1 = 720$$

This is written as 6! or 6 factorial, sometimes called 6 bang.

It would take a while, but eventually you could test all **720 combinations** with **6 desks**. But what about a larger classroom with **24 desks**?

Factorials get big very quickly, and you often need a calculator to work them out. If you have **24 desks** and **24 pupils**, the number of possible arrangements is:

$$24! = 620{,}448{,}401{,}733{,}239{,}439{,}360{,}000$$

If you had been testing one million combinations per second since the beginning of time, you would never get through them all! To finish would take about 20 billion years.

Dividing one factorial by another is not so difficult. For example:

$$\frac{6!}{4!} = \frac{6 \times 5 \times \cancel{4 \times 3 \times 2 \times 1}}{\cancel{4 \times 3 \times 2 \times 1}}$$

That leaves $6 \times 5 = 30$. But what about big numbers? To find the value of

$$\frac{15!}{13!}$$

you don't have to write it out in full:

$$\frac{15 \times 14 \times 13 \times 12 \times 11 \ldots \times 1}{13 \times 12 \times 11 \ldots \times 1} = \frac{15 \times 14 \times 13!}{13!}$$

so that leaves

$$15 \times 14 = 210$$

And we did all that without ever working out the values of either 15! or 13!

Multiplying Factorials

Multiplying factorials is a little tricky, but you only need to find the value of the smaller factorial. For example, to find the value of **8! × 6!** rewrite **8!** as **(8 × 7 × 6!)**. This gives:

$$8! \times 6! =$$
$$8 \times 7 \times 6! \times 6! =$$
$$8 \times 7 \times 720 \times 720$$
$$= 29{,}030{,}400$$

"I don't like sitting here."

Achilles and the Tortoise

In the fifth century BC, the Greek philosopher **Zeno of Elea** posed a series of mathematical brainteasers, now known as Zeno's paradoxes. The most famous involved a hypothetical race between the great warrior and athlete Achilles and a tortoise.

In a race over **10 feet**, Achilles gives the tortoise a 2-foot head start. But Achilles runs at **2 feet per second**, while the tortoise moves at just **1 foot per second**, so surely Achilles will win easily. Zeno suggests that Achilles can never catch the tortoise.

He reasons as follows:
▶ After **1 second**, Achilles will have run **2 feet**. In that time, the tortoise will have moved **1 foot**, so it will be **1 foot ahead**.
▶ Achilles takes ½ **second** to move another **1 foot**, in which time the tortoise will be ½ **foot** ahead.
▶ Achilles takes ¼ **second** to move another ½ **foot**, by which time the tortoise will be ¼ **foot** ahead.

START

After 5 seconds

After 2 seconds

After 1 second

1   2   3

These distances form a series of numbers, each of which is **half the value** of the number before it:

$$2 + 1 + \tfrac{1}{2} + \tfrac{1}{4} + \tfrac{1}{8} + \tfrac{1}{16} + \dots$$

As this series goes on into infinity, it approaches, but never reaches, 4. In Zeno's words:

"In a race, the quicker runner can never overtake the slower, since the chaser must first reach the point from which the chased started, so that the slower must always hold a lead."

Solving the Paradox

A paradox is something that appears logical, but that we know cannot possibly be correct. Zeno's logic seems sound, but it just can't be right. The time periods being considered are also **halving in length** each time:

$$1 + \tfrac{1}{2} + \tfrac{1}{4} + \tfrac{1}{8} + \tfrac{1}{16} + \dots$$

This series approaches, but never reaches, 2. But time doesn't stop. It will click over to 2 seconds, at which point Achilles and the tortoise will be **even at 4 feet**. As time clicks on, Achilles will cross the finish line after **5 seconds**. After 5 seconds, the tortoise will be **3 feet** from the line. Achilles will win easily.

One possible solution to Zeno's paradox of Achilles and the tortoise comes from physics. There may be a **minimum length of time** that can be counted and a **minimum length of distance** that can be measured. It may be that, in reality, as opposed to math, things cannot be divided forever. At some point, the series will come to an end, we will reach the **smallest time** and **length possible**, and Achilles will catch the tortoise.

4　　　　　5　　　　　6　　　　　7　　　　　8　　　　　9　　　

FEET

Fractals

A fractal is a special kind of self-repeating pattern that looks like the same pattern up close as it does from far away.

Sierpinski Triangle

The Sierpinski triangle is a simple fractal that you can draw for yourself.

▶ **Step 1** Start with an equilateral triangle with a solid color.
▶ **Step 2** Draw another triangle by connecting the midpoints of each side of your triangle, and remove the color from this triangle.
▶ **Step 3** Repeat the same process for each of the three smaller triangles.
▶ **Steps 4, 5, etc.** Repeat the process again and again...

The triangle contains a number of fraction series. After Step 2, the fraction of the colored triangle that is left is $3/4$
After Step 3, the fraction left is $9/16$
After Step 4, the fraction left is $27/64$
After Step 5, the fraction left is $81/256$
Each time, the fraction is the square of the fraction before it:
$9/16 = 3^2/4^2$, $27/64 = 3^3/4^3$, $81/256 = 3^4/4^4$
Can you see why this is?

Step 1

Step 2

Step 3

Step 4

This pattern can also be made in three dimensions to form a Sierpinski pyramid.

22

A Fractal Snowflake

Snowflakes are among the many fractal patterns seen in nature.
Here's how to make a six-pointed snowflake fractal.

▶ **Step 1** Start with an equilateral triangle.
▶ **Step 2** Divide each side of the triangle into three equal parts. From each end of the central parts, draw two lines of equal length to make equilateral triangles.
▶ **Steps 3 and 4** Now repeat this same process for each side of your new shape. Repeat again and again.

Step 1   Step 2   Step 3   Step 4

Nature's Fractals

Self-repeating fractal shapes are found all around us. The shape of a tree is a fractal, with branches coming from the trunk, attached to smaller and smaller branches and twigs. Clouds are fractal patterns, which makes it hard for us to tell how far away they are.

Coastlines are fractals. This is the coastline of the Nile delta in Egypt.

Here is a typical Mandelbrot sequence showing the same shape at four different levels of magnification. Zooming in ever closer to the edge reveals self-repeating patterns of great complexity.

This is the shape at least magnification.

As we zoom in, patterns begin to emerge.

Mandelbrot
Magic

Mandelbrot used computer graphics to create and display images of fractal patterns. Clouds or even broccoli, for example, have rough, uneven edges. By repeatedly applying a special equation to each pixel of the image, Mandelbrot was able to show that seemingly **rough or even chaotic** edges actually have a distinct pattern, or degree of order. The exact edge can never be worked out precisely, but the **more** the computer zooms in on the points at the edge, **the finer the detail** becomes.

In the 1970s, the Belgian mathematician Benoit Mandelbrot discovered an extraordinary mathematical set based on a very simple concept. It uses numbers called complex numbers, which include the square root of -1.

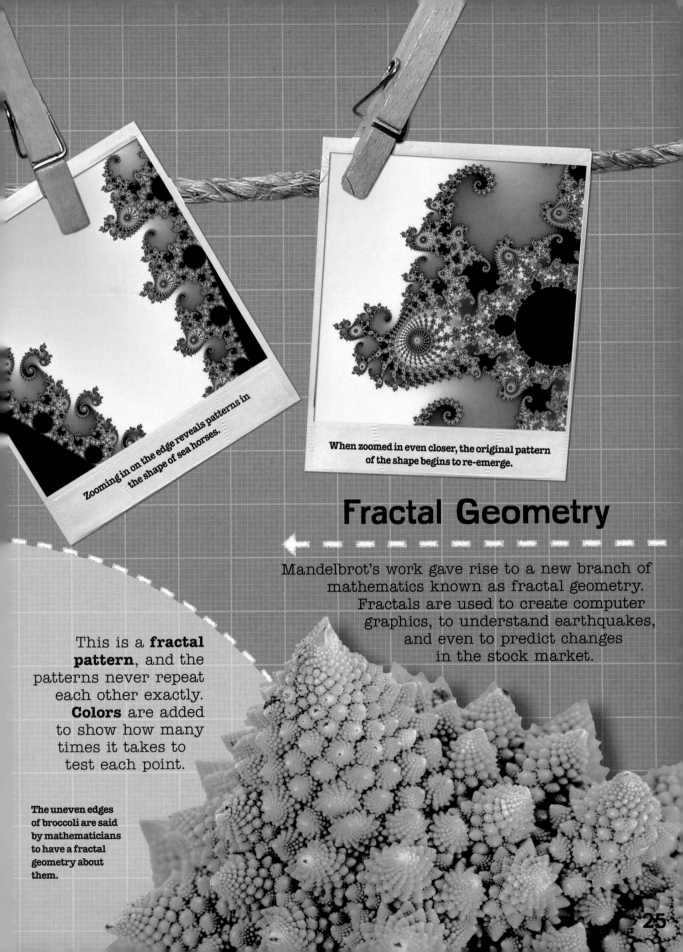

Zooming in on the edge reveals patterns in the shape of sea horses.

When zoomed in even closer, the original pattern of the shape begins to re-emerge.

Fractal Geometry

Mandelbrot's work gave rise to a new branch of mathematics known as fractal geometry. Fractals are used to create computer graphics, to understand earthquakes, and even to predict changes in the stock market.

This is a **fractal pattern**, and the patterns never repeat each other exactly. **Colors** are added to show how many times it takes to test each point.

The uneven edges of broccoli are said by mathematicians to have a fractal geometry about them.

Fooled by a Fraction

The Extra Square

The shape above is made up of the following pieces:

A triangle with height 3 and base 8 (red)

A triangle with height 2 and base 5 (green)

Two L-shapes—one made up of rows of 5 and 3 (blue), and the other with rows of 5 and 2 (yellow)

When you rearrange the shapes so that the **small triangle** is at the bottom, a hole appears as if by magic! **Where has the hole come from?**

The answer is that you have been **tricked**. The red and green triangles are not similar—the red triangle has a height-to-base **ratio of** $^3/_8$, while the green has a **ratio of** $^2/_5$. Finding the common denominator, the ratios are **red** $^{15}/_{40}$ and **green** $^{16}/_{40}$, meaning that the slope of the green triangle is steeper than the slope of the red triangle. The shapes you have made are not quite triangles. Check with a ruler to be sure.

The Smallest Fraction Ever?

Whatever number you can think of, you can always add 1 to make it a bigger number. This means that there are infinite numbers. Infinity is represented in math by the symbol ∞. Similarly, whatever fraction you can think of, you can always make a smaller fraction— $1/\infty$. This is known as an **infinitesimal**, and it is smaller than the smallest number you can think of.

Infinitesimals do not behave like normal fractions. In fact, there is a mathematical proof that $1/\infty = 0$. Here's how it works: The number $1 - 1/\infty = 0.999...$ (that's 0.999 recurring, with the 9s going on forever). See if you can follow it. First, let:

$$x = 0.999...$$

Multiply both sides by 10:

$$10x = 9.999...$$

This can also be written as:

$$10x = 9 + 0.999...$$

That's the same as:

$$10x = 9 + x$$

Subtract x from both sides:

$$9x = 9$$

Divide by 9:

$$x = 1$$

Therefore:

$$1 - 1/\infty = 1$$
$$1/\infty = 0$$

Quiz

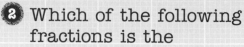

2 Which of the following fractions is the **smallest?**

a) $1/3$ b) $2/5$ c) $4/9$

1 a) If you slice a pizza into **8 slices and eat 3**, what **fraction** of the pizza do you have left?

3 You have a chocolate bar with **12 pieces**. You give **half** of it to a friend, then eat **two-thirds** of the rest. **How many pieces** do you have left?

4 Convert the following **fractions into decimals:**

a) $1/8$ b) $4/5$ c) $1/3$

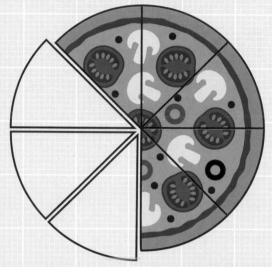

5 Convert the following **decimals into fractions** in their simplest terms:

a) 0.25   b) 0.7   c) 0.111...

b) If you slice two pizzas into **quarters and eat 1 piece** from each, what **fraction of the total amount** of pizza have you eaten?

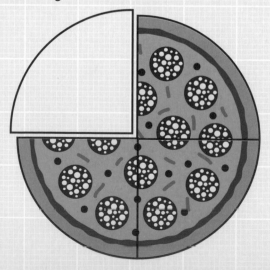

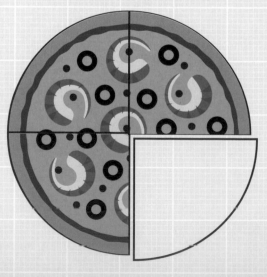

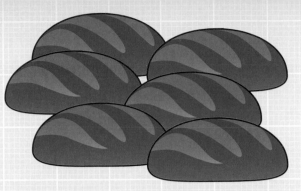

6 For their lunch, **8 workers** have **6 loaves** of bread to share. What is the

minimum number of pieces

of bread you can slice to give **equal shares** to all eight workers?

7 In a sale, all clothes are

reduced in price

by $\frac{1}{3}$. Moira buys a dress, a pair of boots, and a blouse. At full price the dress costs **$60**, the boots cost **$105**, and the blouse costs **$45**. How much does Moira pay **in total**?

8 You are running a market stand where you sell posters, and you have the following expenses: You must give $\frac{1}{3}$ of your earnings **to pay for the stand**. You must give $\frac{2}{5}$ of **your earnings** to the poster supplier. If you sell **30 posters** at **$5** each,

how much

money do you make?

9 Drill-bit sizes are measured in fractions of an inch. The fraction is always expressed in the simplest form. Here are five different sizes:

$$\frac{3}{64}, \frac{1}{4}, \frac{1}{16}, \frac{1}{8}, \frac{3}{32}$$

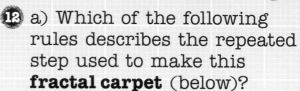

a) Arrange the drill bits in **order of size**, with the smallest first.

b) Drill-bit sizes are sometimes expressed as decimals. If $\frac{1}{64}$ is equal to 0.015625, what are the **decimal conversions** of the five drill-bit sizes, from the smallest to largest?

10 A combination lock has three digits, each from 0 to 9. How many possible **combinations** are there?

11 The following messages have been scrambled into a code by **replacing one letter** with another found next to it in the alphabet. Can you **crack the codes** and work out what they say? What is the **cipher** in each case?

a) L Z S G   D U D Q X V G D Q D

b) T F D S F U   D P E F

12 a) Which of the following rules describes the repeated step used to make this **fractal carpet** (below)?
i) Divide each light square into 9 equal squares and make the middle square dark.
ii) Divide each light square into 16 equal squares and make the 4 squares in the middle dark.
iii) Divide each light square into 9 squares and make the diagonal squares dark.

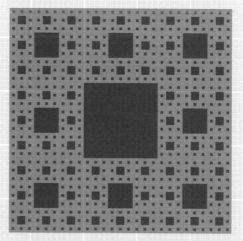

b) If step one creates the first dark square, how many steps are shown in the drawing?

Glossary

Cipher
A mathematical procedure used to produce an encrypted message.

Complex number
A number that contains a term that is a multiple of $\sqrt{-1}$. Also represented as i, $\sqrt{-1}$ is commonly known as an imaginary number.

Cryptography
The study of how to make or break secret codes. The process of turning a message into a secret code is called *encryption*.

Decimal
Describes the number system that is based on multiples of ten. A decimal fraction has a denominator that is a multiple of ten, such as tenths, hundredths, or thousandths.

Exponential rate
Growth that becomes faster and faster as the number that is increasing becomes bigger.

Factorization
The breaking down of a number into smaller numbers that, when multiplied together, yield the original number. Prime factorization breaks a number down into a series of prime numbers.

Infinitesimal
A fraction that is infinitely small. One way of expressing an infinitesimal value is to call it "one divided by infinity."

Infinity
A value that cannot be measured because it goes on forever. It is written with the symbol ∞.

Irrational number
A number that cannot be written in the form a/b, where a and b are whole numbers. $\sqrt{2}$ is an irrational number.

Operation
A procedure to be performed on numbers, such as addition, subtraction, multiplication, or division.

Paradox
A statement that sounds reasonable but that leads to impossible or absurd conclusions. In mathematics, a paradox suggests that at some point you have made a logical mistake.

Reciprocal
The reciprocal of a number is the value that, when multiplied by the number, gives the answer 1. To find the reciprocal of a fraction, you swap the numerator and the denominator.

Series
An infinite sequence of numbers.

Similar
Two objects are similar if they have the same shape, even if they are different sizes. To have the same shape, they must have the same internal angles and the same ratios between the lengths of their sides.

Index

Facts for Now

Visit this Scholastic Web site for more information on fractions and to download the Teaching Guide for this series:
www.factsfornow.scholastic.com
Enter the keywords **Fraction Frenzy**

Answers

1. a) ⁵/₈ b) You have eaten ¹/₂ a pizza. You had two pizzas in total, so the fraction of the total is ¹/₂ ÷ 2 = ¹/₄.
2. a) is the smallest. The lowest common denominator is 45. So: ¹/₃ = ¹⁵/₄₅, ²/₅ = ¹⁸/₄₅, ⁴/₉ = ²⁰/₄₅
3. You have two pieces left.
4. a) 0.125 b) 0.8 c) 0.333...
5. a) ¹/₄ b) ⁷/₁₀ c) ¹/₉
6. Each worker should receive ⁶/₈ of a loaf = ³/₄. Using Egyptian fractions, ³/₄ = ¹/₂ + ¹/₄, so each worker gets one half and one quarter. Four loaves are sliced in half, and two are sliced into quarters. That makes 16 pieces in total.
7. Total cost at full price: 60 + 105 + 45 = $210 Sale price: 210 × ²/₃ = $140
8. Your total earnings are 30 × 5 = $150 The fraction you keep is 1 − ¹/₃ − ²/₅ = (15 − 5 − 6) / 15 = ⁴/₁₅, ⁴/₁₅ × 150 = $40
9. a) ³/₆₄, ¹/₁₆, ³/₃₂, ¹/₈, ¹/₄
b) 0.046875, 0.0625, 0.09375, 0.125, 0.25
10. 1,000
11. a) MATH EVERYWHERE. Cipher: move forward one along the alphabet.
b) SECRET CODE. Cipher: move backward one along the alphabet.
12. a) **i)** b) The drawing shows the fractal after four steps.